40 DEVOTIONS
THAT WORK WITH YOUTH

Edited by
GERALDINE ANDERSON

JBCE

THE JOINT BOARD OF CHRISTIAN EDUCATION
Melbourne

CONTENTS

* Particularly suitable for 12–14 year olds.

INTRODUCTION

'Have you got a creative book of devotions, something I can pick up before my youth group night, know will work and won't turn the kids off?'

After I had been asked that question a few times (and answered that no, we had nothing specifically catering for that) I thought, perhaps we could prepare a book of devotions.

When I thought of the countless devotions I have heard, the impact they have made upon my understanding of God and faith, Jesus and his life, I realised there was an incredible amount of material swimming around in the heads of youth leaders, and people who have worked in all sorts of ways with young people. So why not tap that resource? Why not get these people to put on paper the devotions they have prepared for young people, ones that they know have had an impact and been meaningful?

So here they are — devotions that have been tried and found to be effective. How effective they will be when you use them is up to you. The book is the raw material. You have to develop the basic ideas presented for you in the devotions into your own style, something you can believe in, therefore something your group will be able to catch from you.

The ideas come from a range of people in Australia and New Zealand. Make them yours.

The devotions in this book are suitable for youth in many settings, be it the end or start of a youth group night, during a camp or as part of a worship service.

It is important, however, that you assess whether or not these devotions are suitable for your group. It is up to you to decide what you can use with the young people you know.

Geraldine Anderson

PREPARING DEVOTIONS

A devotion for a youth group, like any other act of worship in the church, requires certain components. These components are essential to the devotion to make it truly worship.

We have asked people experienced in leading devotions and worship with youth groups what they thought a devotion should contain and be about. Some of their opinions are noted below:

A devotion should contain a message which challenges young people, which lets them feel an awareness of God and gives them a chance to respond in faith.

A devotion should relate the Bible to life issues, stressing the importance of worshipping together, being a friend, standing alongside those who need help.

A devotion should challenge young people with faith and ask them to make radical commitments to the gospel.

A devotion should be short, sharp and punchy with a strong message.

A devotion should include, as a matter of course, prayer, biblical input, individual reflection, a challenge, and an awareness of God.

A devotion is not a humanistic story; it is an act of worship. Therefore the prominent message coming through must be one with spiritual significance. This is not to say that a devotion cannot talk about life issues; it is saying that these life issues should be bound up with Jesus' teaching, his life style, challenging young people all the time with the Christian message.

THE DEVOTION

It is important for a group to know when a devotion is to begin; sometimes just announcing the start of a devotion is not enough to settle the group down and get their minds away from themselves and on to God. Therefore there must be a clear starting point, that is, a call to worship.

There may be a special room or part of the hall you can go to that the members know is set aside for devotion and worship. Or you might use a focus for worship, or worship centre, such as an open Bible, a cross, a candle, a poster or picture, a floral arrangement.

You might like to take the group to the very front of the church, sit them on the floor and begin worship from there.

You might play a taped song (the same each time devotions are to begin) or sing a few lively choruses, ending in some soft, settling songs. Again these give the group members a chance to bring themselves into a worshipful frame of mind.

It is important for the leader of a devotion to know where he/she is going to stand. Try not to change the focus of attention too much by having people popping up from around the room to read from the Bible or read a poem. Focus the group's attention on one spot and work from there. In this way the members will listen to what you are saying rather than be distracted by what is happening around them.

A point to remember is: the larger the number of people you have, the more formal you must be. By that, I mean you must have a sound structure within a large group, plus guidelines of what is appropriate in worship. If you are working with a small group, you can afford to approach worship less formally, asking for opinions, suggestions for songs, etc. Therefore, suit your style of worship to your group.

Make the devotion important. Make it reverent and serious. Constantly remind the group that they are worshipping God. Give them time to reflect upon God — time to get out of the experience of the group's activities and change their focus and attention from themselves and their friends to God.

Don't be afraid to stop occasionally and explain elements of worship like confession and forgiveness etc. Also, while reading the Bible, stop to explain parts that people may find confusing. This can only add to any worship experience.

Give clear directions to participants about what they have to do. For example, tell the people who are to read or lead the singing at what part of the devotion they are to come in.

When choosing a devotion, try to use one which will fit into the night's (or day's) activities. This will help keep a flow of events. For example, if you are planning a 'Futuristic' night, use 'Where are you going to?' on page 16.

PRESENTING THE ELEMENTS OF A DEVOTION

There are different ways of presenting the components necessary for a devotion, for example:

Different ways to read from the Bible: Use a reading choir, three or more people who take a verse each of a Bible passage and read in consecutive order. Use the Bible as a storytelling resource; put the verses into your own words and tell it like a story. There are many songs, the lyrics of which come straight from the Bible; use song to deliver the biblical message.

Different ways to sing: Have a small choir able to sing reasonably well teach different songs to the group. Ask the group to look out for new songs to teach to the others. Sing in rounds: sing joyfully and with feeling, sing quietly and with reverence. Use actions to suit the words of lively songs.

Different ways to pray: Use open or spontaneous prayer, that is a prayer which is left open to the group, so that they might pray for their concerns and needs. Pray by looking into the eyes of the people within the group. Pray silently while playing meditative music.

ONE IMPORTANT POINT

The young people within your group need to know that worship is not a group exercise, focusing on life issues only. Worship involves focusing attention on God and his will for us. As a leader of devotions, you must see to it that the members of your group remove themselves from the fun and laughter of their group experience and give God the attention. You can be as creative, different and dynamic as you like as long as you keep the basic elements essential for worship. And most importantly, never lose sight of the fact that you are worshipping God.

ABOUT THIS BOOK

Devotions marked * in the Table of Contents are especially useful with 12–14 year olds.

Many hymns recommended by title are from the *Australian Hymn Book* (Australia)/*With One Voice* (New Zealand). They are abbreviated AHB/WOV.

The Bible is needed for each devotion.

GREETING GOD AND CREATION

(especially suitable for mornings)

PREPARATION

You will need: a person to read the words of the Gloria.

DEVOTION

Start by singing a loud exuberant hymn or song of praise.

Have a member read the words of the Gloria, this is one of the oldest songs of praise in the history of the Christian Church.

Glory to God in the highest,
and peace to his people on earth.
Lord God, heavenly King,
almighty God and Father,
we worship you, we give you thanks,
we praise you for your glory.

Lord Jesus Christ,
only Son of the Father,
Lord God, Lamb of God,
you take away the sin of the world:
have mercy on us;
you are seated at the right hand
of the Father;
receive our prayer.

For you alone are the Holy One,
you alone are the Lord,
you alone are the Most High,
Jesus Christ,
with the Holy Spirit,
in the glory of God the Father. Amen.

Have the members go outside and find any object of nature — for example a leaf, a stick, a stone, a flower, some grass — and return immediately.

Have the members observe their objects, look at features, individual characteristics, beauty or ugliness, see how it was created.

Leader: The objects you have in your possession at the moment are created by God. Think about that, look again at the fine detail of the object you have. Now think of this: we are also created by God, and God can see us and know us in great detail, just as we can see and know the object we have.

Read Psalm 139:1–6.

Sing 'Let us sing to the God of salvation' (AHB/WOV no. 115).

Have the members get into groups of six or seven. Have them place their objects into the centre of the small group. Then have everyone select a different object, not their own. Tell the members that they are to quietly watch who picks up their original object. Next time the group meets, they are to look out for the needs of that person.

Then pray, committing the day and the group to God.

Finish with a blessing of dispersion: Go out into the day, look afresh for God, for what he has made is good, and he has made you. Praise God with your heart and your mind and in all your actions. Amen.

Andrea McAdam

POSSESSIONS

PREPARATION
You will need: two people for a role play, one person for a Bible reading.

DEVOTION

Leader opens with prayer: Let us pray. Jesus, help us to understand the things you have taught us. Open our hearts to your real message as we come to worship. Amen.

Introduce the role play by saying: I want you to imagine a scene which we will briefly act for you. A developer (that is, someone who believes in using and developing resources) is strolling along the shores of a lake in an underdeveloped country. He comes across a fisherman, basking in the sun.

Developer   Why are you not out on the lake fishing today?

Fisherman   I caught many fish yesterday, enough for today and tomorrow. I do not need to fish today

Developer   But if you fish today, you will get more money.

Fisherman   Why would I want more money?

Developer   Well, if you had more money, you could buy a new high-powered fishing boat.

Fisherman   Why would I want a new high-powered fishing boat?

Developer   With a new boat you can catch ten times more fish and make ten times more money.

Fisherman   But what is the use of ten times more fish and ten times more money?

Developer   With the extra money, you can buy yourself a large palatial home, with a big swimming pool and many luxuries.

Fisherman   What would I want with a big house and swimming pool?

Developer   Once you get a few possessions, you will be wealthy and soon you will never have to work again.

Fisherman   But what is the use of all this?

Developer   So that you can spend your days just basking in the sun

Fisherman   But isn't that what I'm doing now?

Have a member read Matthew 6:24-34.

Lead the group in discussing or reflecting on these questions:
What are the qualities of the developer?
How materialistic are you?
What do possessions mean to you?

What are the qualities of the fisherman?
What are the similarities of the fisherman's qualities to the qualities Jesus asks us to have in Matthew, chapter 6?

Finish with an appropriate song such as 'Seek ye first the Kingdom of God'.

Or use this prayer: Lord, help us to put our trust in you, not to worry about the food we need to stay alive, or about the clothes we need for our bodies. We will try to trust that you know what we need and that you will provide. Help us to be concerned more with your kingdom here on earth and your everlasting love. Amen.

Geraldine Anderson

FRIED EGGS

PREPARATION

You will need: paper, pencils, scissors, masking tape, a member to read a Bible passage.

DEVOTION

The leader should tell the following story as if it were his/her own:

I was walking down the main street of town one hot January day. It was about 40 degrees, and the streets were full of hot sticky people. Suddenly, coming towards me, I saw a thin little woman, wearing an old baggy dress with little white daisies all over it. And on her forehead was a fried egg. Now I thought it was fairly unusual to see this woman, because the people with the fried eggs on their heads don't usually come out until September or October. Anyway there she was, this lady with the fried egg on her head. As I watched her, I prayed, 'Oh God, please don't let me wake up tomorrow and want to put a fried egg on my head'. I passed by her, stopped, and like many other people, turned and watched her walk on. Then I prayed, 'Oh God, if by chance I wake up tomorrow and want to put a fried egg on my head, please don't let anyone see it. And if they do see it and they want to laugh about it, let them laugh, but please don't let them laugh so that I can hear.' Because

the truth about fried eggs, you can call it a fried egg or anything you like — a problem, a strain, is that everybody's got one. Some people wear it on the outside, some people keep it on the inside.

Leave some time for reflective silence.

Direct the members to break into groups of two or three. Ask them to draw a fried egg and cut it out.

Ask the members to talk to the others in their group about how they react when something is troubling them or when they have a problem. Do they hide their feelings or do they show them?

Ask them to write some of the things that worry them on their fried egg. Supply the members with some masking tape and offer them the opportunity to stick their fried eggs on their foreheads. The leader *must* ensure that the members have a chance to decline the offer if they so wish.

Bring the group back together (with their fried eggs on their foreheads) and give them a little time to read others' concerns.

Conduct an open prayer. The leader might start the prayer by asking for help when we are troubled.

Finish by having a member read Psalm 13.

Geraldine Anderson

OOH, THAT SMARTS!

Suitable for 12–14 year olds)

PREPARATION *You will need: four or five packets of Smarties, depending upon the size of your group, one packet of Smarties per seven people.*

DEVOTION

Start with a few well-known choruses e.g., 'Allelu, Allelu','Come let us sing', 'Doing it all to the glory of God'.

Introduce the theme:
Ask the members if they know what the word 'temptation' means, and have them explain it.

Perhaps ask for a few stories from the members about when they have been tempted to do something they shouldn't.

Divide into groups of seven. Give a packet of Smarties to one person in each small group. Indicate that under no circumstances are they allowed to eat any of the Smarties. However, they are to tip the contents of the box into their hands and examine the Smarties.

Tell them to look for colour, design, smell, feel. Then they are to put the Smarties back into the box and hand them on to the next person. They repeat the procedure. Make sure you stress to the group that they are not allowed to eat the Smarties; they are just allowed to look at them, feel them and smell them.

When everyone has had a turn, have the Smarties brought back to the front.

Then ask these questions:
What did it feel like, having the Smarties so close, yet not being able to eat them?
How did you feel when someone else had the box?
Did you watch everyone else to see if they ate any Smarties?
Did you feel like sneaking a Smartie?

Then read Matthew 4:1–11.

Finish by saying the Lord's Prayer together.

Peter Taubner

PRAYER

PREPARATION
You will need: newsprint, masking tape, felt pens, and the following Bible verses on separate pieces of newsprint:

1. *When you pray, do not use a lot of meaningless words, as the pagans do . . . Your Father already knows what you need before you ask him. (Matthew 6:7–8)*
2. *After sending the people away, he went up a hill by himself to pray. (Matthew 14:23)*
3. *Don't worry about anything, but in all your prayers ask God for what you need, always asking him with a thankful heart. (Philippians 4:6)*
4. *Speak, Lord, your servant is listening. (1 Samuel 3:9)*
5. *The Lord said to him, 'Go, because I have chosen him to serve me . . .' (Acts 9:15)*
6. *When you pray and ask for something, believe that you have received it, and you will be given whatever you ask for. (Mark 11:24)*
7. *Be joyful always, pray at all times. (1 Thessalonians 5:16–17)*

Put the verses on newsprint in different parts of the room.

DEVOTION

Start with a well-known chorus, one for which the group does not need books.

Ask the members to get up and go around the room and read every verse on the pieces of newsprint.

Ask them then to pick the one verse that says the most to them about prayer. Give them about three minutes and ask them to stand near the one they have chosen. Have the members discuss with people who have picked the same verse why they chose that verse.

Then have members get into pairs with someone who chose differently to them and discuss each person's choice.

Have the group gather together again and tell them how *you* feel about prayer, and which verse you would have picked and why.

Finish in prayer, inviting the members to open their eyes and look around at the other members in the group while listening to the words of the prayer: Lord, we come before you in prayer, knowing you are listening. We know sometimes we don't pray as often as we should, and when we do pray, we tend to get it over and done with quickly. Help us to spend more time with you in prayer, to talk with you and bring the day's trials and joys to you. (Leave some time for personal prayer.) Please be with us as we continue our lives, watch over us and keep us safe, through Jesus Christ our Lord. Amen.

Anne Harley

THE LIGHT OF THE WORLD

PREPARATION *You will need: a small candle for each person (like the ones used on birthday cakes) and a slightly larger candle for the leader.*

DEVOTION

Have the members seated in a close circle. Light the leader's candle and turn the lights out.

Leader: Jesus said 'I am the light of the world. If you follow me, you shall not walk in darkness.'

Sing a song about Jesus the light.

Lead a prayer of confession. Let us pray: Lord, we know that today we have not been perfect. We know we have sinned, we know we have disregarded the teachings of Jesus. We may have turned our backs on someone in need, been unfair at home or at school or work, put someone down easily and without a second thought. Please forgive us, Lord, forgive our weaknesses, forgive our selfishness. And now we pray our Lord's prayer . . . 'Our Father . . .'

Read John 1: 1–5.

Light the candle of the person on either side of the leader, and let the light be passed progressively round the circle.

Sing a song of praise.

Finish with a blessing: Go in peace, in the knowledge that the Christ-light will never falter and never leave you in darkness.

As the group moves away, some people may like to sit apart for a while. Be sure that the group is sensitive to this.

Andrea McAdam

WHERE ARE YOU GOING TO?

DEVOTION

Start with a well-known chorus, one about directions or pilgrimage.

Give out paper and pencil to each person and say:
   Write three words that you would use to describe yourself.
   Write three words a parent would use to describe you.
   Write three words your best friend would use to describe you.
The leader might like to have the questions written on newsprint.

Ask the members to reflect in silence, to look at the nine words written and to think honestly about who they really are and what they are really like.

Then read the following story expressively and clearly:

John Cartmill had never been to Singapore before. His flight arrived at 4:30 p.m., and having cleared customs, he went direct to the Hotel Royal into which he had booked (in writing) some three weeks previously. Entering the hotel foyer he approached the attendant, introduced himself, and requested h room number and key.

'But Mr. Cartmill', the attendant replied, 'you already have your key. I gave it to you around 2:00 p.m. You went straight to your room on the third floor, No. 313.' John Cartmill's first reaction was to argue. He had never been in this hotel or Singapore before. He certainly hadn't picked up his key at 2:00 p.m.

Curiosity, however, began to take over. He picked up his case, went to the lift and rode to the 3rd floor. It didn't take long to locate Room 313 and briefly pausing, he knocked on the door and waited. The sound of footsteps were clearly heard and the door opened.

There in front of John was a man who looked almost identical to himself. A little greyer, a few more crinkles around the corners of the eyes, a little more weight . . . but otherwise just like himself.

John Cartmill had met himself as he would be, ten years from now. He entered the room and they began to talk . . .

The leader should allow some time for silent reflection.

Then encourage the members to think about where they are going by reading the following:

If we could meet ourselves ten years from now, who would we meet?
   Some of us will have finished school

and study and be in well-paid, secure jobs.
Some of us may be unemployed.
Some may be married.
Some may have children.
Some may already be divorced.
Some may still be part of the church.
Some may even have died.
Some may feel happy, and as if life has meaning and purpose.
Some may feel as if they've really blown it.
Would we be proud of the person we'd meet? What would they tell us to avoid?

Leader: What we become is determined by the decisions we make *now*. That is, the things we do, the friends we make, the place God is allowed in our lives. Listen to what the Bible has to say about this.

Have a member read Ecclesiastes 11:9 to 12:7.

Leader: Let us pray. Lord, help us in our lives to strive towards something you want us to be. Help us to become the people you have planned us to be. We give thanks for your love and support. Help us to make the right decisions, with your support. We ask these things, assured you are listening. Amen.

Finish with a well known chorus, one for which the group does not need song books or word sheets.

Graham Johnson

THE BALLOON OF ENTHUSIASM

PREPARATION

You will need: a balloon for each person, plus a few extras, a felt pen for each person, some newsprint, a member to help you with a demonstration.

DEVOTION

Ask the group to brainstorm some synonyms for the word 'ENTHUSIASM'. Write the thoughts on newsprint.

Read Acts 2:1–4, 17–18.

Then say: The word enthusiasm comes from the Greek word meaning filled with God's spirit and power.

Take a look at this balloon. You can blow it up quickly, by filling it with air (have a member demonstrate this) and you can deflate it just as quickly by letting all the air out.

Our enthusiasm rate is much the same as this balloon. We are quickly fired up about some things, then are just as quickly bored or lose our initial zest and become deflated. (The leader should give out the balloons, asking members not to fiddle with them.)

I want you to blow up your balloons; keep them blown up, but don't tie a knot in them. Just hold them for a while. Imagine the balloon is your body and the air is 'enthusiasm' —

God's power. Sometimes when doubts come along and you feel that God has deserted you, you tend to deflate. So the best thing to do is to tie a knot in the top of your enthusiasm outlet (direct the members to tie a knot in their balloons) so that it can't escape. Sometimes someone may come along with a pin and burst your balloon, letting all your enthusiasm escape.

So if it bursts, just come and get another balloon, fill it up, and tie a knot in the top. There are balloons just waiting to be filled with God's power and love. (The leader should give out felt pens to the members.)

Now I want you to write your name on your balloon. Stand up and throw it into the air. Make sure you catch someone else's balloon. (When all has settled down again, continue.) You've now got someone else's balloon, someone else's enthusiasm.

We are charged, as Christians, to spread our enthusiasm and share God's power and love with the people who are around us.

Make sure that you remember that a balloon, like human emotions, is a fragile thing and often bursts. But there are always more balloons to fill, just as there are many ways that God helps us and heals us.

The leader finishes in prayer: Lord , in a world where no one seems to care, where sometimes apathy reigns, help us to be enthusiastic Christians, wanting to serve. Amen.

Geraldine Anderson

ODDS AND ENDS

DEVOTION

Have the members sit in a circle on the floor.

Place the set of everyday objects in the centre of the circle. Ask the group to look silently at the objects and choose one which represents something about what the group means to them or how they feel about the group. (You may have to give examples here, such as: The battery might represent being 'recharged'. The aspirin might mean the group gives them a headache, sometimes.)

Give about three minutes to choose. Then go around the group and have members individually pick up their items and share why they chose them. The item should then be replaced so that another person can use it.

An alternative is to hand out plasticine, and have people make their own symbols of what the group means to them.

Then read a passage from the Bible about Christian fellowship, either one of the following three, or one of your own choosing: Colossians 3:12–17, Ephesians 3:16–21, Philippians 2:1–11.

Finish in prayer. Begin by asking members to hold the hands of the people sitting next to them. Ask them to look at the people on each side of them, the people whose hands they are holding. Tell the members there will be a time during the prayer when they will be directed to pray for the person on their left, and on their right.

Prayer: Lord, there are many good things about our group, but we know your presence with us is the best thing we have. Help us to care constantly for the people in our group, to love and support each member as you have taught us to. We would now like to pray for the person sitting on our left (leave one or two minutes in silence). Lord, hear our prayer for the person sitting on our right (leave one or two minutes in silence). Lord, hear our prayers and help us through the coming week, until we can come together in your name again. Amen.

Craig Mitchell

ARE YOU FEELING LOST?

PREPARATION *You will need: three different translations of the Bible and three members to read them.*

DEVOTION

Have the members with the Bibles read the three different translations of Matthew 18:12–13 separately.

Then ask the members to get comfortable, perhaps by lying on the floor or getting more comfortable in their seats.

Leader: Think back to a time when you have felt lost:
Lost for words . . .
Lost for what to do . . .
Lost in other situations . . .

What did you feel? (pause)
What did you think? (pause)

Now consider these questions:
What did you do?
Who helped you,
or found you,
or how did you find your way ahead?

Read the meditation on the next page.

Leader: Here is something else to think about.
There are many people in our society who are lost. As a response to God, try something radical and make a friendship with a person or group that is disadvantaged, or hurt or lost. Consider the life of Jesus as your model.

Remember to share what you do with a friend and with God.

Finish by singing: 'Make me a channel of your peace' or use the prayer of St. Francis (page 47).

Mike Armour

Meditation

God
the beginning
the one who says I am who I am,
Creator,
Life giver,
the one who sustains us
and is the essence of our being,
who loves us beyond our words and
imaginations,
mountains rise in your glory,
valleys descend to guide our paths
and the whole of your creation
shows us
the wonder of your presence
among us.
You seek to change us
to be your people.
You make and remake us
in your image,
and challenge us to follow you
along narrow winding roads,
up steep hills,
across rushing rivers
and through all the turmoil
that embraces our lives.
You call us to be
thinking
dreaming
feeling
touching
loving
caring and
reaching out to those
who hurt, who are alone, who suffer
and who need to feel your presence
and love.
You say you will use our lives if we
trust you,
and we are afraid because
we hurt, we are alone,
and we feel rejected;
and yet in our weakness, our fear,
our frailty and our lostness
you come looking
to find us and bring us home
so we can care and love.
We need you, we need each other,
we need to break down the barriers,
smash through the stereotypes
that keep us apart
and allow you to live in our lives
so that we can be your life to others.
We are like lost sheep,
like clay for the potter's wheel.
Find us and mould us
and use us in your world,
for the sake of Jesus.
Amen

MY GOD AND MY HANDICAP

PREPARATION

You will need: one person for a Bible reading. Have the members sit on the floor in a circle, an arm's length away from each other.

DEVOTION

Read the following story to the group:

Meredith Allan developed a crippling disease in 1969. Because of this she underwent extensive brain surgery in 1969 and 1970 in order to control the continuous and exhaustive abnormal movements of her body.

Meredith is now 22 years old; she is unable to speak, yet she has complete understanding of written and spoken speech. Her control of her limb posture and limb movement is permanently disturbed. Her writing is extremely difficult and laborious and her disability is such that she will never be able to work with her arms or perform any work which requires her to be on her feet or walking. Meredith lives in Glen Waverley in Victoria. This is her statement, written in 1981 — the International Year of the Disabled.

I was brought up to believe in God, and with all the creation about me on my parent's farm, it was hard not to believe.

When I started getting ill and my body was in permanent torture, my faith seemed to grow, not to lessen. When I didn't know what was going on around me and what was happening to my body, I'm sure God was there with me.

I was put into the Austin Hospital in Melbourne for two weeks and six days of diagnosis. After all that, they still couldn't be sure what was wrong with me. After six months of not knowing myself, it was strange having 200 doctors not know either.

Then I was put into St. Vincent's Hospital under the most wonderful doctor, whose faith in God, complete humility and total confidence in me shatters me now when I look back. To explain his strength, I have to explain a day in his life. He was a neurosurgeon, worked all day operating, and at 2:00 p.m. this day started a nine hour operation on me and visited me at midnight when I was back in the ward. At 8.30 the next morning, he was back wanting to see Mum and Dad. Later we found out he was called in at three in the morning for an emergency. With a man like that operating, what could I do but put my total faith in God and him?

The first operations were done in 1969. I was to have waited six months before the next two operations. But when I was sick with pain in May, I went back into hospital. It had only been three months since the first two operations; my doctor said he needed to wait six months before he operated again.

My parents had been told I had two months to live before I kicked myself to death, due to the abnormal movements of my body. I wanted to tell them that I was not going to die, that God would not let me die. And even if I did die, I wanted them to be happy that I was out of pain. Somehow I couldn't find the strength to tell them.

My doctor ended up doing the two operations within ten days, creating medical history. The next day, Mum and Dad had a conference with my doctor and in that, they asked him, 'Why?' He answered simply, 'God told me to'. Mum and Dad still remember how at that moment they looked up at the picture of the praying hands on his wall.

I was cured of my disease; however the handicaps I have now are from operation damage. I was left like a vegetable after the operation; I couldn't move a muscle. It was a month before I could laugh! Gradually, six months later, I learned to walk again and it was four years before I could wink.

I went to Yooralla, a school for the disabled, and boarded there. Then I went to Balwyn High School, gained my Higher School Certificate, and I am now at Monash University doing third year arts. I know that without God, I wouldn't be where I am now.

The hurtful remarks passed at me don't seem to hurt as much when I know God is sharing them with me. I do get depressed, but God is the only one who knows how bad the depression gets, thank goodness.

Of course, I wish I was (so-called) 'normal', to be able to eat properly without choking, to be able to swim properly. However that is all vanity and every day I thank God for my life, the friends I have made, and the wonderful experiences I have had. I am grateful for my life and even more thankful that I live in Australia. Although Australia is not perfect and we have a long way to go, I am faced with the reality that if I lived in 140 of the 150 countries of the world, I would have had no chance to live.

Ask the members to discuss these questions with one other person:
  What sort of faith does Meredith have?
  What sort of faith do you have?

Have a member read Mark 5:25–34.

Ask the members to reflect upon these questions:
  Are there any similarities between the woman who touched Jesus' cloak and Meredith?
  What does Jesus say to those who have great faith in him?

Finish in prayer: Lord, help us to have great faith, to conquer all odds and believe as the biblical woman and Meredith do. Help us to understand your power, wisdom and love. We ask that you nurture us in our faith. Amen.

Geraldine Anderson

PASSAGES

(For any time of farewell, especially when one or several young people are leaving the group)

PREPARATION

You will need to have four people for the reading choir, people who can read aloud fairly well. They will need copies of their parts and practice ahead of time. You will also need one large candle and small ones for each person, and a cake large enough to serve everyone.

DEVOTION

Reading choir: (The number 1–4 should be assigned to individuals, with each reading the appropriate words or sentences)
(1) Bye!
(2) See ya.
(3) God bless.
(4) Don't forget to write!
(1) Take care.
(2) So long.
(3) Be good.
(4) Hurry back.
(1) Drive safely.
(2) Keep in touch.
(3) Shalom.
(4) Adios!
(1) We'll miss you.
(2) Love ya!
(3) Bon voyage.
(4) Farewell.
(1) Call when you get there.
(2) Peace be with you.
(3) Come back soon.
(4) Goodbye.

Leader: Passages are times in our lives when we move from one thing to another, from one stage or time to another. Birthdays are passages. Weddings are passages. Leaving school, or home, or a group of friends are other passages. Passages are times of sadness and times of joy, with the mixture of what's old and familiar and what's new and exciting and unknown. Just after Jesus and his disciples had the Last Supper together, he told them that he would be leaving them soon. Listen to that story.

Bible reading: (Have the reading choir read John 13:31 to 14:31. One person should be the narrator and read all the parts not in quotation marks. One person should read the words of Jesus, another person those of Simon Peter and Judas, and the fourth person the words of Thomas and Philip.)

Leader: Jesus said that he would be separated from his friends, and that he would die. But he also said that he would be with them in a new and different way — through the Holy Spirit, the Helper — and he gave them a new command to love one another in the same way that he loved them. Even though he wouldn't be with them as he had in the past few years, he would be with them in another way. One way to think about this is by using candles. This candle represents Jesus and his presence. We can light our candles from it, and even when the Jesus candle is put out, the light is still there. We make the light shine by following the command to love one another.

Song and candle lighting: Sing 'A new commandment' or 'You light up my life'. While the singing is going on, have each person, one at a time, light his/her candle from the Jesus candle. At the end, extinguish the Jesus candle.

Leader: It's a bit the same when someone leaves us today, or makes a passage into a new time of life, a new place, a new group. That person or those people may not be with us in the same way, but their light still shines for us, when we remember them. Wherever they are, their lights are shining partly because of the time we have spent together. Passages — for instance, birthdays or weddings — often are celebrated with cakes. We have one now, a passage cake of farewell. And even though we may not be happy about saying goodbye, we can be happy about the good new things ahead for all of us. We can be happy, too, about the light shining wherever we are. (Cut and distribute the cake; eat it.)

Prayer: Goodbye is our shorthand version of saying, 'God be with you'. God, be with us now. We are sad because people we love are leaving, and we are afraid we will be lonely. We will miss them. We know that time and space will turn faces into memory, and letters and telephone calls will have to substitute for constant presence. This makes us sad. Even if we may see each other often, it just won't be quite the same. But we can find some comfort in knowing that with you, Lord, it is never goodbye. You are present with us when we meet together, through your Word and through the sacraments. You are the spirit that links us up with those who are leaving us. When we miss each other, and the presence of the others, help us to remember the message of the candle light. Help us to give the same love we have for the one (or ones) leaving to the one (or ones) who will be joining us. God, be with us. Amen.

Leader: It's time now to say goodbye. Remember that goodbye means 'God be with you'. (Ask the one or ones who are leaving to go to the door and stand there. Have the one or ones leaving say, 'God be with you' and those leaving saying, 'And also with you'. Then have the one or ones leaving actually depart.)

Leader: When Jesus did leave his disciples, the Bible tells us that they kept looking at the place where they had last seen him. Two messengers came along and said, 'Why are you standing there looking? He will be back, as he said.' It was time for the followers of Jesus to get on with the work he had given them to do. And it's time for us to do the same. Goodbye. God be with you. (The group replies: 'And also with you'.)

Mary-Ruth Marshall

25

DOUBTING

PREPARATION

You will need to think a little about your faith, perhaps discuss it with your minister or a friend before doing this devotion. Doubt is something many people face; it is up to you to decide whether you want to present yourself like this to your group.

DEVOTION

Sing a song about faith and love.

Have a member read John 20:24–29.

Leader: Sometimes, I am a little like Thomas. I think to myself 'If only I could have been there to see Jesus, to talk to him, to touch him, to ask questions of him, then everything would be much easier to understand'.

Let's go back to Thomas. Thomas was one of the original twelve disciples; surely he should have been the first one to believe that Jesus had risen from the dead. He at least had eye witnesses telling him they had seen the Lord. But why did he doubt? Perhaps because Thomas was the kind of man who couldn't believe without seeing. He had cut himself off from the other disciples because he was bewildered and hurt at Jesus' death. He was told the good news, but couldn't believe it, didn't dare to hope.

Sometimes, I am a little like that. I daren't hope, it all seems so good,

almost as if I should have to earn God's love rather than just ask for it.

Three outstanding points arise from the Thomas story for me which give me that hope and courage to go on believing in Jesus Christ. They are: that Jesus did not blame Thomas for his doubts. Jesus knew that once Thomas had fought his way through his doubts he would be sure. Also, Jesus blames no-one for wanting to be sure. Rather he says not to profess a faith of which you are not absolutely sure, and you must fight like Thomas fought until you reach certainty. And finally, Thomas gives us the hope and strength to believe when, after he had seen Jesus, spoken to him and touched him, he said with conviction and certainty 'My Lord and my God!'

When I doubt, I rather like to think of Thomas whose first reaction was not to do what he was told to do and not to believe what he was asked to believe. But once he was convinced he believed with certainty. Thomas and I have made a discovery. That discovery is one that every Christian makes — that by ourselves many things are impossible, but with God nothing is impossible.

Sing a quiet song about knowing Jesus.

Finish in silent prayer. Leave about two or three minutes for the members to offer their prayers to God.

Geraldine Anderson

ANY OLD PORT IN A STORM

(suitable for 12–14 year olds)

PREPARATION
You will need: a record album cover, a school textbook, a camera, a cricket bat or tennis racquet, a saucepan and a very large Bible. You will also need something that will cover them up — a suitcase or a sheet. Two members are needed for Bible readings.

DEVOTION

Invite a member of the group who goes to school to come to the front to help you. Shake his/her right hand, **but don't let go**.

Reach for the record cover without letting anyone see it. Ask if the volunteer appreciates music. Whether the answer is yes or no, hand him or her the album cover. (He or she will have to hold it in the left hand.)

Next, ask if he/she goes to school. (Naturally the answer is yes: give him or her the text book.)

Again, ask if the volunteer plays a sport. Whether the answer is yes or no hand the bat and/or racquet to him/her.

About this time you can let go of the volunteer's hand so that he/she can hold everything easily. Continue handing out things until all that is left is the Bible. The Bible should be the biggest, heaviest Bible you can find.

Ask the volunteer if he/she attends Sunday school or church, and give him/her the Bible. If you plan it properly, and have enough items, the volunteer won't be able to hold everything, and the Bible will fall away.

Leader: Sometimes our hobbies, or work, or holidays, or sport, cloud our image of God and we lose hold of him, but if we have him first, everything fits in nicely.

The leader should help the volunteer restack the items. The leader should give the volunteer the Bible again and help him/her stack everything on top of it. The stack should remain secure, if you help a bit. You might like to point out that the hand of God can steady us (as you are steadying the stack) if we let it.

Ask the volunteer to sit back with the rest of the group.

Finish by having two members read Matthew 19:26 and Mark 9:23.

Peter Taubner

REALISM

PREPARATION

You will need: three drawings, one of a dancer, one of an artist, one of a singer. Have these on an easel and turn each one over, face down, as the story unfolds.

DEVOTION

The leader should read the following story clearly and with feeling.

When I was young I desperately wanted to be a ballet dancer. So my parents enrolled me in a class at the local dance studio. My teacher thought I had a huge future if I continued practising. I dreamed of dancing like Fonteyn, and perhaps joining the Australian Ballet Company. But everybody told me that I was being unrealistic and I was dreaming. They said that the world of dancing was too tough to get into and that I would never make the big time. After a while I agreed — I was being unrealistic, my goal was above my abilities, so I gave it up.

Then I wanted to be an artist. I painted whenever I got the opportunity. My art teacher and I thought I had a huge future if I could keep at it and accumulate enough paintings for an exhibition. But everybody told me I was being unrealistic, that I was dreaming. They said that Da Vinci and Rembrandt were the REAL painters, that I couldn't possibly reach any sort of standard that hasn't been reached before. After a while I agreed I was being unrealistic, painting was only for great people who had done all that could be done in the art world, so I gave it up.

I became very interested in singing and decided that this was the career for me. I went to singing classes, formed my own band, sang contemporary and traditional songs at parties and weddings for friends. My singing teacher and I thought I could probably be a big success in the singing world. But everybody said I was being unrealistic. Didn't I know what a demanding scene the music world was? Didn't I know that everybody wanted to be a singer? That singers were a dime a dozen? After a while I agreed I was being unrealistic — great singers like Melba, Crosby, bands like the Beatles were legends never to be usurped, I could never compete in their world, I was just ordinary, so I gave it up.

Now I am a trained librarian. I sing in the shower, avidly read all that comes into the library on art, and go to the ballet at least twice a month, and everyone says I'm a realist.

Ask the members to divide into groups of two or three and discuss these questions:
As a child what did you say you wanted to be when you grew up?
What do you think your parents would

like you to be?
Have you ever wished you could be famous, clever, wealthy, good at dancing, singing, acting, painting etc? Why?

Call the group back together, and have a member read Romans 12:1–2.

Finish with a few lively choruses.

Geraldine Anderson

BOND

PREPARATION *You will need: newsprint with a cross drawn on it, felt pens, one between two people; and three people to read from the Bible.*

DEVOTION

Begin with a prayer: Lord, we come into a time of worship, knowing you are with us. Open our ears, hearts and minds to your word and message. We give thanks for this time together, the opportunity to worship you. We respond by praising your name and all you do and have done for us. Amen.

Sing a song seeking God's strength.

Put the newsprint with the cross drawn on it into the middle of the group. Invite everyone to trace one hand onto the newsprint — not onto the actual cross but around it.

Leader: What we have done with this cross is to create a bond — a bond with each other and a bond between Christ and us individually, and as a group. We have gathered ourselves around the cross, we have joined with Christ in his suffering. As the cross is also the sign of the church, we are creating an alliance with the church, Christ's church. The actions and messages of Jesus are part of us. We take on the duty of witnessing to the world. But what is most important is that we do it with each other and under the sign of the cross.

Have the three members read John 3:16, Matthew 28:16–20 and 1 John 3:11, 16–18. When each Bible reading is completed, write inside the cross where the reading comes from (e.g., John 3:16).

Leader: In the Bible readings we have heard about the purpose of Jesus' life on earth, what is possible for all people and something of the power available to us through God. We are told about our calling as people of Jesus, bonded together, worshipping one God. And we have heard something of what our attitudes towards our brothers and sisters should be — the response to the fellowship of Jesus we have entered into.

Read the Apostles' Creed in the *Australian Hymn Book* or *With One Voice*.

Sing a benediction to end.

Mark Lawrence

IMAGINE

PREPARATION *You will need: the song 'Imagine' from the* Imagine *album by John Lennon. (This is optional.)*

DEVOTION

Have the members lie down and get as comfortable as they can. Ask them to close their eyes. Leave some time so that the last fidgeting is over before you start. Soften the lights and then start.

Leader: In the beginning God created heaven and earth . . .
Imagine that . . .

Imagine nothing.
Can you?
Or is our world too concrete to see how that is possible?

It takes a little imagination (pause)
to see how the story of creation
all comes together
with land and sea, animals, plants —
and people.

The story says we are created in God's own image . . . (pause)
Does that mean we look like God?
Think like God?
Act like God?

To answer those questions you'll need some more of that imagination (pause).
If you can imagine that people were created in the image of God, then it's not very difficult to see where our imagination comes from.

We use our imagination every day, whether we recognise it or not. Can you think of some times when you have used your imagination? (Leave some time.)

I think we can use our imagination in two ways:
1. To meet our own needs — and these may not necessarily be selfish.
2. To respond to the God within us, by using our creativity, our imagination, to share with others.

Listen to John Lennon's song 'Imagine' and see if there is any relevance to living a Christian life in the 80s. (Play or read the song if you wish to.)

The prophet Micah wrote some wise words about our response to God (chapter 6, verse 8). 'No, the Lord has told us what is good. What he requires of us is this: to do what is just, to show constant love, and to live in humble fellowship with our God.'

Imagine what our world would be like if we could all respond to God like this . . . (Leave some time for reflection.)

Finish with an open prayer. The leader should start by asking for forgiveness because we don't always do what is just and loving.

Mike Armour

FLYING FREE

PREPARATION

You will need: the music 'Dear father, number 2' from the album Jonathan Livingston Seagull *by Neil Diamond. Alternatively you could use some classical music, something which has a floating, flying quality about it.*

DEVOTION

Open in prayer: Lord, we've come to listen to you, hear your word, respond and bring ourselves a little bit further in our faith journey. Open our ears and hearts. Help us to use times of silence wisely so that we hear you and understand your will for us. Give us this chance to let our thoughts and prayers fly up to you. Amen.

Leader: Hang-gliding is a sport which appeals to many people, but only a few people take part in it. When you hear what is needed to participate in this sport, you may understand why few people embark upon it.

The hang-glider requires equipment, for example the glider itself, all the safety gear, transport to get to the area of flying and time.

When actually beginning to fly, the hang-glider will need to know the basics of how to run, how to hold the frame, where to fly from and when, and at what moment he/she should take the biggest step of all — jump off the cliff top.

Whilst in the air, the hang-glider needs to sense the wind currents, listen to the changes, the pull and different movements of the glider. He/she is not actually controlling the glider, but being guided by the forces. Yet the hang-glider must be constantly aware. Once all this has been achieved, the hang-glider will be flying free.

The hang-gliding experience can be related to us on our Christian journey. Let's look at the equipment needed, not in a material sense, but in a spiritual sense.

The equipment we need is our friends, the church, our family, people to support us. We need resources like the Bible, so that we have a foundation to build on, just as the hang-glider needs the frame of the glider to fly.

One of the biggest steps in hang-gliding is the jump off the cliff. The glider needs an incredible amount of trust in him/herself and the elements to be able to take that first step. Our trust is based on our faith. We need to make that very first step of faith when we commit our lives to God. We need to step forward and say we trust God and entrust our lives to him.

So now that we've 'jumped off the cliff' we are in the air. The hang-glider listens to changes, feels the wind currents and is guided by his/her senses. God will be our source of movement when we finally make it into the air, he will be the one we will have to listen to, we will have to let the Holy Spirit take over and guide us.

Once all this has been attained, we fly free with God.

Read Galatians 5:1, 13–16.

Leader: As Christians our freedom involves a certain responsibility. We need to love one another, love God and then we are free, free to fly with God.

Leave some time for silent reflection.

Then have the members relax themselves, perhaps they might like to lie on the floor, or get a little more comfortable in their seats. Play the music you have chosen to play, either the classical music or the piece from *Jonathan Livingston Seagull*. Tell the members they are to let their minds fly free with God, either in prayer or silent thought.

Finish in prayer: Father, guide us in your direction, make us sensitive to changes and give us faith in you that involves our whole mind, body and soul. Let us grow in this journey to love one another day by day. In your name we ask this. Amen.

Wendy Leversha

THE GREATEST THING IN THE WORLD

(suitable for 12–14 year olds)

PREPARATION

You will need three people to do a role play. Rehearsal is necessary. The characters are: two earthlings — Bill and Fred (normally dressed) and a being from outer space (weirdly dressed) — Zurk.

DEVOTION

Have the role players present this drama.

(Bill and Fred are deeply involved in conversation — whispering — Zurk approaches them slowly, watching them carefully.)

Fred: *(looks up and sees Zurk; startled)* Hey, Bill, look at that!

Bill: Aahh!! What is it?

Zurk: Don't be afraid; I won't harm you. I come from another world many light-years away. We — my companions and I — had to make a landing on your planet. We have to carry out minor repairs on our space ship. We will soon be finished and on our way again.

Fred: *(still a little frightened)* B-b-but you speak our language.

Zurk: Yes, your brain waves are easily deciphered.

(Bill and Fred draw close to each other to discuss in whispers. Zurk looks around him and finally comments.)

Zurk: Yuck, what a terrible place; it's dead and dull. How do you ever live here?

Bill: You mean here on earth? Why it's easy. There's lots of fun things to do and see.

Zurk: Like what?

Fred: Well, we've got T.V.

Zurk: T.V.???

Fred: Yes television. It's like a box, with a screen and people appear on it and entertain you. It's terrifific.

Zurk: Huh! Why back home we have 'instant experiences'.

(Bill and Fred look puzzled.)

Zurk: It's like your T.V. only it's three-dimensional, and much better. You just select the experience of your choice, and whammo, you're there. Not only seeing and hearing it, but actually involved in it.

Bill: Boy! *(pause)* But we've got a lot more things besides T.V. We've got cars, and trucks, and planes, and . . .

Zurk: Cars?

Bill: Yes, it's like a smallish metal box, with wheels and a motor and comfortable insides. It takes you quickly from one place to another.

Zurk: Bah! Why back home, it's all instantaneous. Select the co-ordinates of your destination, press the appropriate button, and you're there — just like that! *(snaps his fingers)*

Fred: Wow! *(in desperation)* But we've also got planes that go through the air, and rockets that go out into space . . .

Zurk: Look at my space ship! How do you think I got here, anyway?

Fred: Yeah, forgot about that.

Zurk: Come on — surely you must have something worthwhile on this planet?

(Bill and Fred start discussing in whispers)

Zurk: *(after a while)* There must be something you have that we don't have!

We know — Jesus Christ!

Zurk: *(repeats)* Jesus Christ???

Bill: *(slowly)* Yes, he is the Son of God and is himself God, too. He came down to this planet and lived here as a man! He came and died to save us from our sins, to bring us back into a loving relationship with his father, so that we too can be God's children!

Zurk: *(amazed and incredulous)* You mean to say that Almighty God, the God who created the whole universe, came to *this* planet?!!

Fred: That's right.

Zurk: And actually *died* for you??? *(Walks off slowly, shaking his head)*

Sing a quiet song about knowing Jesus.

Finish in prayer: Lord, thank you for your son Jesus, for his love and kindness. Help us to let him into our lives, and recognise him for what he is — the greatest gift given to humanity. Amen.

Jeff Deuble

JESUS' STORY AND MY STORY: THE FIRST 15 YEARS

(suitable for 12–14 year olds)

PREPARATION

You will need: newsprint, felt pens, masking tape. You will need to write out the questions on newsprint so that the members will be able to read and refer to them while they are in their groups.

DEVOTION

Organise the members into groups of four or five.

Read Luke 2:1–7, then ask these questions:
  Where were you born?
  What effect has that location had on you and your family?

Read Luke 2:8–20, then ask these questions:
  Who announced your birth?
  What words would you use to describe your mother?

Read Luke 2:21 and Matthew 1:21, then ask these questions:
  Where does your name come from?
  What is your nickname?
  What is the significance of a person's name?

Read Luke 2:22–38, then ask these questions:
  Were you baptised?
  Where was your baptism?
  What promises were made?
  What has been the continuing effect of your Baptism/dedication?

Read Luke 2:39–40, then ask these questions:
  Where were your early years?
  What were your father's/mother's occupations?
  How have those years influenced your life?

Read Luke 2:41–52, then ask these questions:
  Who influenced you most during your childhood?
  What were the unhappy times of your childhood?
  Did Confirmation/confession of faith come easy, difficult, not at all?
  What helped/hindered that?

Then bring the group together again and sing a well-known chorus, one which the members will not need books for.

Finish with a prayer: Lord, we have looked at our lives and Jesus' life. We know that we were hardly anything like the boy Jesus. Help us to follow in his footsteps as we reach adulthood; help us to be like him, kind, loving, caring, just. We thank you for his example and pray that we will be able to be examples for the children to come. Amen.

David Grant

OUT IN THE COLD

(a winter devotion)

PREPARATION
You will need: to gather some statistics about the number of homeless people in Australia, New Zealand or your city, and the temperature lows for the past few nights.

DEVOTION

Before the devotion begins, ask the members to take off their coats and jumpers and go outside and stand in the cold. They should not touch anyone else or speak. After a few minutes, the members should come back inside, put on their coats and warm each other up.

Encourage the members to huddle together in a large group for warmth, sitting together on the floor. Then signify that the devotion is to begin by saying a phrase such as 'Let us begin our time of devotion'.

Read out the gathered statistics.

Encourage the group to talk with the people around them about how **they** felt in the cold.

Have a member read the following poem:

ON THE SWAG *

His body doubled under the pack
that sprawled untidily on his old back
the cold wet deadbeat
plods up the track.

The cook peers out,
'O curse that old lag,
here again with his clumsy swag
made up of a dirty old turnip bag.'

Bring him in cook,
from the grey level sleet,
put silk on his body,
slippers on his feet,
give him fire and bread and meat.

Let the fruit be plucked
and the cake be iced,
and the bed be snug
and the wine be spiced
in the old cove's nightcap,
for this is Christ.

The leader should then present a challenge to the group, stating the responsibility of a Christian to care for those who are destitute, needy, ill and imprisoned. Alternatively, ask the group to suggest what practical ways they might help those who are cold, hungry or homeless.

Finish by singing 'When I needed a neighbour' AHB/WOV 558.

At the end of the song, leave some time for silent reflection. Then signify that the devotion is at an end.

Scott Finlay

* From *Collected Poems* by R.A.K. Mason. Published by Pegasus Press, New Zealand. Used with permission.

A TIME

DEVOTION

Sing a few lively choruses.

Indicate that you are entering into a time of devotion, and that the devotion will begin with a brief time of silence for personal prayer. After some time, finish the prayer time by saying: Lord, open our hearts and eyes to you during this time of devotion. Amen.

Explain to the members that the song 'Turn, turn, turn', by Pete Seeger, is based on the Bible passage, Ecclesiastes 3:1–8 (you might like to sing it if you have the words and music).

Read Ecclesiastes 3:1–8.

Have the members think about what kind of time it is for them at this moment. It may be a time referred to in the reading, or another time such as a time to study, a time to plan for the future, a time to make a big decision, a time to make a new friend etc. Then read the Bible reading again, this time very slowly.

Ask the members to share with one other person 'times' that they thought of, that are relevant to them at this moment. Indicate that the members may choose not to share.

If time will allow, provide an opportunity for the members who wish to, to share their 'times' with the whole group.

Finish in prayer: Lord, help us to know what time it is for us. Help us to know what your will for us is at this time. Help us to allow enough time in our busy lives to keep in touch with you. We ask these things in your name. Amen.

Grant Nichol

REFLECTION ON PARALYSIS

PREPARATION
You will need: a member to read a poem.

DEVOTION

Have everyone sitting upright in a chair, more than an arm's length away from anyone else. Ask them to close their eyes and to imagine that they have been in an accident and are paralysed from the neck down.

Have the members hang their hands down by their sides, stiffen their bodies so they feel uncomfortable and place their feet flat on the floor, tensing their leg muscles.

Then help them 'feel' their immobility; ask them to reflect on these questions in silence. Give about half a minute after each question for reflection.

How does it feel to know you can't use your arms and legs?

What things are you now unable to do by yourself?

How does it feel to need help to change, shower etc?

How will your paralysis affect your friendships, your job hopes, your future?

Ask members to keep their bodies stiff and uncomfortable, then guide them through these reflections:

Imagine your best friend is right next to you. See his/her face. By some miracle your friend says to you, 'I'll take your place. I'll spend the rest of my life in that wheel chair, I'll set you free.' How does that make you feel towards your friend?

Now, instead of that friend, see the face of Jesus telling you, 'I will take your place'.

Then have someone read the following poem:

I'm trapped!
Entwined in a steel cocoon;
Motorised motion, where once I leapt and ran;
chained inside my future;
locked in fear and desperation,
imprisoned by self pity.
Who could hold the key
to release my sinking soul?

'Have my strong legs', he said,
'To skip and dance and leap for joy.
Have my hands, to touch and hold,
clasped in prayer

and lifted in praise.
Be new and whole, and abundant of life!
For I will wear your shackles of despair;
take on your yoke of crushed ambition;
lie captive in your ties of grief.
Be free again!'

And there he lay — paralysed,
in my place.
Feet and hands stilled to move
no more.
Feet and hands nailed
to a splintered tree.
He was captive to my false ambition;
chained by my foolish pride;
a prisoner of my self-indulgence.
He bears the stain of my 'fall'
And I am free!
How great his love for me!

Direct the members to relax, to feel their limbs again, slowly flex their muscles.

Sing a song about Jesus suffering for us.

End in prayer: Lord, you said you would be here to share all our sorrows; you died for us, you took our place on the cross. We want to thank you and praise you for your love. Help us to follow you, try to be like you and love as you love us. We ask these things in your name. Amen.

Craig Mitchell

MY CHURCH IS BETTER THAN YOUR CHURCH

PREPARATION *You will need: four members to help with a role play. Rehearsal is necessary. You will also need someone to read a Bible passage.*

DEVOTION

(There are four characters: 1, 2, 3 and 4. All four are arrogant and short in their speech. They should line up in a straight line facing the group. They should stand in consecutive order.)

Script

1: *(looks directly into eyes of 2; 3 and 4 look straight ahead)* My church is better than your church!

2: You don't say!

1: I do say. My church is better than your church!

2: Oh yeah! Tell me all about it.

1: We have three full-time ministers, more members than any other church in our district, a full congregation at all three of our Sunday services, a huge cathedral-type building, waiting lists for our Sunday school classes, five youth groups and the best family dinners this side of heaven! Top that! You with your little store-front church, struggling each week to pay your part-time minister. You don't even look like a church should look. My church is better than your church!

(1 looks straight ahead; 2 looks into the eyes of 3.)

2: My church is better than your church. We may be small, but we have spirit. No stuffy formalised prayer and responsive readings for our people. Every service the place is electric with excitement. People clap, shout 'Amen' and sing so loud the ceiling shakes. My church is better than your church!

3: Yuck!

1: *(still looking ahead)* Yuck is right!

2: Someday, you big institutionalised churches will wake up to the truth. You think the church is a business instead of the temple of the Spirit.

(1 and 2 look straight ahead; 3 and 4 face off this time.)

3: *(speaking to 4)* My church is better than your church. We have the TRUTH. We are the real truth. There are many churches, but **the** church is right here, with people like me. You shouldn't even be calling yourself the church unless you believe what we believe; and from what I hear, you don't. There's not room for the both of us in the church. One of us better leave and it sure isn't going to be me! My church is better than your church!

4: *(back to 3)* Well you go ahead and get all excited about the truth, but you haven't convinced me. My church is still better than your church. We have the friendliest people anywhere. Our minister is a plain ordinary guy, not bad-looking either. And talk about a nice give-and-take community where everyone does their part. It's a nice place to be, our church. Couldn't ask for a nicer bunch of people. My church is better than your church.

1: *(to group)* It's the numbers!

2: *(to group)* No, it's the spirit!

3: *(to group)* It's the truth!

4: *(to group)* You're all wrong, it's the people!

ALL *(pointing their fingers at group)* My church is better than your church!*

Have a member read Mark 9:33–37.

Sing a few choruses about unity and being one in the Spirit.

Leader then finishes in prayer: Lord, help us to remember your commandment, that we love one another. We know that in your eyes, we are all equal. No one is better than the other. Help us to realise that whatever church we belong to or whatever stands we take, we do it for

you, not simply for numbers, spirit, truth or people, but for you. Amen.

Geraldine Anderson

* Reprinted from RESOURCES FOR YOUTH MINISTRY, a quarterly publication of the Board for Youth Services of the Lutheran Church, Missouri Synod, 500 N. Broadway, St. Louis, MO. Used by permission.

LET YOUR BODIES TALK

PREPARATION *You will need: to make sure you understand the body sculpture exercise.*

DEVOTION

Have the members sitting on the floor in a circle, leaving a large space in the middle of the circle free.

Leader: I would like to create a body sculpture with this group. Firstly I'd like (pick a person) to come into the middle of the circle and strike a pose which expresses the way he/she feels at the present time. (After the person has moved around a little tell him/her to freeze his/her position.)

Now I'd like to invite you all, one at a time to join on to this person, creating your own sculpture with your body. (Invite one member at a time to join onto the sculpture. This can be done fairly quickly if you tell people to 'freeze' when they have got into position.)

Have the members remain in place while you read: Ephesians 4:1–6, 11–13, 16.

When the reading has finished, have the members relax their poses and sit down on the floor where they are. Ask the members if they felt uncomfortable at all. Were they supporting people or being supported by someone else?

Then say: Now I'd like you to reflect upon your position in the 'sculpture'. Where did you fit in? Were you on the fringes? Were you right in the middle, surrounded by your friends? Did you feel as if the group had created 'one body'?

Sing a rousing chorus such as 'Side by side'.

Finish in prayer: Lord, we are people from different places, with different ideals, dreams and aspirations, yet we know, if we work hard at it, we can be one body, united by your spirit. Help us to remember the words of Paul as he wrote to the Ephesians: 'Live a life that measures up to the standard God set when he called you. Be always humble, gentle and patient. Show your love by being tolerant with one another. Do your best to preserve the unity which the Spirit gives by means of the peace that binds you together.' Grant us your wisdom, Lord, to strive towards creating one body of humankind, so that we may worship you and follow the example you have set. Amen.

Ian Crawford

CANDLE, CROSS, BIBLE AND BALL

PREPARATION
You will need: three members to read from the Bible, a small table, a plastic ball, a cross, an open Bible, a candle. (Arrange these on the table so that the candle-light throws the shadow of the cross across the Bible and the ball.) Seat the members in a circle (facing inwards).

DEVOTION

With everyone seated around the table and the candle lit, turn out the lights. While everyone focuses their attention on the worship centre, sing a quiet but well-known chorus.

The leader introduces one minute of silent meditation during which everyone is to focus their thoughts on what the worship centre depicts for them. The leader encourages everyone to turn to the next person and briefly explain what they see and its meaning to them. (Allow a few minutes.)

The leader asks the members to state what the message of the worship centre is. (Some responses have been: 'I see the candle is like Jesus.' 'The ball is like the world/earth and he sheds his light over the cross and Bible into the world.' 'The cross too has a light and dark side to it.')

The leader should allow these to proceed and where appropriate clarify and reinforce the gospel message that emerges.

Three members then read the following Bible passages:
John 8:12
1 John 1:5–10
Mark 8:34–35

If the group is one which is used to impromptu prayer, have the group offer appropriate one sentence prayers. If the group is not used to impromptu prayer, have three prayers prepared:
Thanks for Jesus, the one who brings light and hope to our world, and to us individually.
Prayer for our world and its dark spots.
Prayer that we may be willing to take up our cross.

Graham Johnson

THE SALT OF FRIENDSHIP

PREPARATION

You will need: an old brown paper bag and a clean white paper bag, as described below, a container of salt, a loaf of bread, and a large plastic bag. Put the salt and the bread in the plastic bag. You will also need someone to mime the story while you tell it, and two people to read Bible passages. You will need to practise the story and the miming ahead of time. To prepare the shopping bags, print the words 'share', 'care', 'grow', 'touch', 'listen', 'love' and 'yes' in large clear letters on pieces of paper or cardboard. Place them in the old brown paper bag. Draw a shoe on both sides of the white paper bag, and print the words 'no', 'ignore', 'don't', 'mine' and 'who cares' in large clear letters on pieces of paper or cardboard. Place them in the white paper bag.

DEVOTION

Begin by placing the plastic bag containing the salt and the bread somewhere where all can see it. Then have the following passages read by two members: Job 6:6, Matthew 5:13.

Tell or read the following story, with a member miming the actions as you describe them.

A lady named Olive owned two shopping bags full of words. One bag was plain brown, very old, and filled with the kind of words that could reach out and connect her with other people. *(Olive holds up brown bag, takes out the words and displays them to group.)* Words like **share** and **care**, **grow** and **touch** and **listen** and **love** and **yes**. *(Olive returns words to brown bag.)*

Olive's other shopping bag was white with a big shoe printed on the sides of it. *(Olive holds up white bag, takes out the words and displays them to group.)* This bag carried words to keep people away. Words like **no** and **ignore** and **don't** and **mine** and **who cares**.

Olive carried both shopping bags everywhere with her. But she only used the connecting words on very special occasions like Christmas or somebody's birthday. *(Pause while Olive gives out words from brown bag to members of group, together with elaborate and insincere hugs, then takes words back and returns them to brown bag.)* The separating words, on the other hand, were used every single day. Olive used them well. She flung them about like darts whenever someone got too close. *(Pause while Olive throws words from white bag at group.)* After a while people moved away without a word.

One day as she was walking to the discount store Olive's plain brown shopping bag broke and spilled out all its words. *(Pause while Olive tears brown bag and spills words out onto floor.)* Suddenly Olive was connected to everyone around. And it wasn't even Christmas. *(Olive collects words from floor, and passes them out to group members.)*

Allow a few moments of silent reflection.

The leader says: Olive's words in the brown shopping bag, words like share, care, listen and love, were something like the food without salt, or the salt that lost its saltiness, that we heard about in the Bible readings. They were the right kinds of words, but they didn't have the right flavour. Maybe they had no flavour at all. The whole idea of being like salt is used quite a bit in the Bible. For the people of those times, salt was almost indispensable. They lived in a very hot climate, so they used salt to keep their meat from spoiling. Salt was also used with their sacrifices, as a sign of purifying. But most important, salt (which was precious and rather expensive) was a sign of hospitality. If you ate the king's salt, you pledged absolute loyalty to him. To eat bread and salt with someone else was to make an unbreakable pledge of friendship. So when Jesus, and other people in the Bible, talk about being like salt that keeps its saltiness, they are using a kind of shorthand language meaning being loyal and faithful, and having a distinctiveness about what you are and do.

Jesus was talking to his disciples one day about this idea of being distinctive and true to yourself and what you believe. After he talked about salt as a way of purifying, and salt being useless if it loses its saltiness, he said to his followers, 'Have the salt of friendship among yourselves, and live in peace with one another'. (Mark 9:50) Having the salt of friendship means backing up words like care and listen and share with sincere action: not just talking about caring, but really caring, not just talking about listening, but really listening to one another.

We have an opportunity now to make a pledge of friendship to one another by eating bread and salt together. It's a way of saying we will have the salt of friendship among ourselves.

The leader then takes the bread and salt from the bag, and passes it around the group, inviting members to break off a piece of bread, dip it in some salt and offer it to the next person.

The leader says: Let us pray. God our father, help us to be salty Christians, distinctive and giving flavour to our own lives and to those around us. Help us to connect with others, and to listen, love, share, care and grow. Give us the salt of friendship for one another and help us to live in peace. Amen.

Mary-Ruth Marshall

(The parable 'A Lady Named Olive' is by Pat Ryan. It is reprinted with permission from *alive now!*, March/April 1978, copyright © 1978, The Upper Room.)

COMPASSION

PREPARATION *You will need: three candles, two members to help with Bible readings.*

DEVOTION

The leader darkens the room and has two members read the following Bible passages by candlelight: Zechariah 7:8–10, Malachi 3:13–18.
The leader should then read the following story by candlelight:

In 1941, 20,000 German war prisoners were to be marched through the streets of Moscow. The pavements swarmed with onlookers, cordonned off by police. The crowd was mostly women — Russian women who had borne half the burden of the war. Every one of them must have had a father or husband, brother or son killed by the Germans. They gazed with hatred in the direction from which the column was to appear. At last they saw it.

The generals marched at the head, looking with contempt at the people in the crowd. The women were clenching their fists. The policemen had all they could do to hold them back.

All at once something happened to the women. They saw German soldiers, thin, unshaven, wearing dirty bloodstained bandages, on crutches or leaning on the shoulders of their comrades; the soldiers walked with their heads down.

The street became dead silent — the only sound was the shuffling of boots and the thumping of crutches. A woman pushed forward and touched a policeman's shoulder saying 'Let me through'.

She went up to the column, took from her coat something wrapped in a coloured handkerchief, and unfolded it. It was a crust of black bread. She pushed it awkwardly into the pocket of a soldier, so exhausted that he was tottering on his feet.

And then suddenly, from every side, women were running towards soldiers, pushing into their hands bread, cigarettes, whatever they had. The soldiers were no longer enemies, they were people.

The leader should blow out his/her candle.

The members who read from the Bible should read their passage again, each blowing out his/her candle when finished.

Leave some time for reflective silence.

The leader should then invite the people to pray for help in their struggles to be just and merciful, to give thanks for those people who overcome prejudice and are able to be merciful and compassionate, and to thank God for his love, mercy and grace.

Geraldine Anderson

PLAYING GAMES

(suitable for 12–14 year olds)

DEVOTION

Leader: We all play games at some time or other. I'm not talking about chess or volley ball; I'm talking about those times when we aren't really honest with ourselves and others.

Take for example:
That friend at school or work who's always acting 'tough'.
The girl who dresses and tries to act as though she's five years older.
The pop star or celebrity who makes out they 'have it all together' on the screen and stage, but their personal lives are altogether different.
The Christian who acts religious on Sunday, but is different at home, school, work or among friends.

Why do we play these games? Why do we often try to be somebody we're not? I believe that many times it's not because we are deliberately trying to be dishonest or deceitful, but because we are afraid:
Afraid of what other people may think if they really know our inner thoughts and motives.
Afraid that people may not accept us just for ourselves. So we try to be somebody they won't reject.

For the same reason, many people try to play games with God. Remember when Adam and Eve sinned in the garden of Eden? They were afraid and their guilt caused them to play games. First they tried to play 'hide and seek'. Then they played pass the buck (Adam said, 'It's not my fault — it's the woman's because she gave me the fruit'. Eve said, 'It's not my fault — it's the snake's because he tempted me'.) But how crazy it is to try to pull the wool over God's eyes. He knows all. He knows us even better than we know ourselves. And I believe he wants us to be open and honest with ourselves, others and him. It's only when we are true to him that we can begin to experience his love, and the forgiveness he is wanting to give us.

Sing a well known chorus.

Then pray the prayer of St. Francis of Assisi:

Lord, make me an instrument of your peace:
where there is hatred, let me sow love;
where there is injury, pardon;
where there is doubt, faith;
where there is despair, hope;
where there is darkness, light;
and where there is sadness, joy.
O Divine Master, grant that I may not so much seek
to be consoled as to console,
to be understood as to understand,
to be loved as to love.
For it is in giving that we receive,
it is in pardoning that we are pardoned,
and it is in dying that we are born to eternal life. Amen.

Jeff Deuble

MEETING JESUS

DEVOTION

Sing some quiet songs together. Introduce a short time of silent prayer.

Leader: This devotion will give you an opportunity to listen to what God is saying to you. Too often when we pray, we do all the talking so God can't get a word in.

I'd like you to get as comfortable as you can, either sitting in a chair or lying on the floor. However don't get so comfortable that you are likely to fall asleep.

Read Mark 1:16–20.

Leader: Take yourselves in your minds back 2,000 years to the time of Jesus. Imagine you are in a boat in the middle of the sea of Galilee (pause). Picture the cliffs around the lake (pause), the shimmer of the sun on the water (pause), watch and listen to the waves breaking against the boat (pause), feel the movement and swaying of the boat (pause), the wind in your hair (pause), the burning sun on your face (pause), the spray of the waves breaking against the boat (pause). Listen to the sound of the creaking of the boat (pause), the sound of the wind (pause), feel the roughness of the boat (pause) the coolness of the water as you place your hands in it (pause).

The boat is approaching a sandy beach which can be seen in the distance. There is a tiny figure on the beach. Watch the figure closely as the boat moves closer and closer to the shore (pause). You are now close enough to make out that the figure is a man. Watch him closely as you draw nearer (pause). The man appears to be waving to you. You can now see him clearly. Picture what he looks like (pause). The boat is now ten yards from the beach, and touches the sand. You climb out of the boat, and feel the sand between your toes. You pull the boat up the beach a little which takes some effort (pause). The man now beckons you to come over to him (pause). You walk towards him, watching him as you move (pause). You are now close enough to see that the man is Jesus. You know that he knows what is on your mind at the moment (pause). He speaks to you (pause). What does he say? (pause). You answer him and continue the conversation in your mind. (Allow a short period of silence.) You finish the conversation with Jesus, and you slowly bring yourself back to now. (Allow some further time for the group to 'come back' to the present.)

Encourage members who wish to, to speak to one other person about their experience. Finish with a time of open prayer.

Grant Nichol

THAT WE MAY HAVE LIFE

PREPARATION

You will need: copies of the Australian Hymn Book or With One Voice and the picture on page 49.

DEVOTION

Sing some quiet meditative songs, for example 'Yesu, Yesu' AHB/WOV 561, 'Living Lord' AHB/WOV 451.

Begin with a prayer: Father, we come before you knowing you are with us and can hear our prayer. Open our hearts to your message, guide us in our thoughts and deeds and steer us in the direction you wish us to follow. We ask these things in your name. Amen.

Show the picture to the group and hold it up while speaking. Everyone should be given a chance to see the picture. While still exhibiting the picture read the following meditation, written by Peter Moss, until recently head of the World Council of Churches Youth Sub-Unit in Geneva.

I'd like to invite you to join me in meditating on the face of Christ. Consider the face. Take some time and look at it carefully. See what strikes you or touches you inside. Spend some time and let yourself be open to a new understanding of the suffering of our God. (*Leave a few*

minutes for the members to look at the picture.)

When I first looked at the face, I was struck by the beard and the hair. A full healthy beard. It looks good, a sign of strength. The hair is somehow different. Long and straggly, it seems unwashed, unkempt. It has not been cared for recently. Either he is not taking care of himself or he has not been allowed to. There seems to be some emptiness there, some lostness or lack of control.

Then I noticed the thorns, the 'crown' of thorns. I suppose I had never thought very much about it, at least not in detail. But here there is no escaping it. The stems are thick, strong, interwoven with each other, firmly wedged on the head. The thorns are long, pointed, vicious, like predators seeking their prey. And at his forehead they sink like claws into his flesh. I am shocked at the piercing and the blood running down the forehead, nose and chin, even falling like great drops of sweat into oblivion. The face shows the strain, the pressure of what is happening, of the monstrous injustice which is being carried out. A face once strong and alive has been reduced to one of submission and suffering.

While I was looking at the face, I was interrupted and it was some time before I came back to it. In the meantime, I was looking through a publication when I came across a drawing of a man — naked, arms stretched apart, body taut and in reat pain. It was not a picture of Jesus, nor of anyone being crucified. was an illustration of the 'parrilla', escribed by Amnesty International s the 'most effective torture'. A wo-tiered 'bed' of wire-mesh is overed with plastic; electrodes are connected to many parts of the body specially nipples, eyelids and genitals and the victim tied down while electric shocks are administered.

The British government has restored full diplomatic relations with Chile and lifted the embargo on British arms sales to Chile — claiming that the human rights situation has improved. Yet the government acted just when Amnesty International was receiving reports of a resurgence of torture in Chile. The 'parrilla' occurs again and again in these reports. So, while the Chilean and British governments proclaim that things are improving, men and women are stripped (like Christ), stretched out (like Christ) and tortured by those claiming to defend Christian civilization.

It was hard to look again at the face of Christ. It was no longer the face of one man alone, but the face of each person tortured on the 'parrilla' or by any other means, the face of each person unjustly executed or murdered.

And the thing that now strikes me most about the face is that the eyes are closed. Eyes are very important for me, a means of communicating, often deeper than words or other gestures. There were no eyes like those of Jesus. They must have been the deepest eyes which other people could ever be invited to look into and to experience. But now they are closed — it is too late to look into and draw strength from them. I was shaken. I felt as if someone had hit me in the stomach. I kept looking at the eyes but they would not open. It was too late, the chance had gone.

Then, only faith is left. Only the faith that the witnesses have spoken truly, that the cross was not the end, but only the death which had to be endured for the resurrection to come. And if he is risen then we can look into not only his eyes, but his whole being, with which by grace we are allowed to come into communion. At the moment of triumph on Easter morning let us all commit or re-commit ourselves to work for the rights of all people and peoples, in the name of the One of whom we say: 'Christ is risen: He is risen indeed'.

Signify that the members may have some time for silent reflection. Then conduct an open prayer.

Finish by singing a resurrection hymn from the *Australian Hymn Book* /*With One Voice.*

Geraldine Anderson

SHARING BREAD AND FISH

PREPARATION

You will need: to be by the beach, or a lake, or a river etc. You will need enough fish to feed the members in your group, and some bread, perhaps rolls for each person. A small fire will need to be lit.

In your preparation, consider having the fire well lit before the members come down to the waterside, and the fish cooking.

DEVOTION

Have the members settle around the fire and the cooking fish. Sing a few well-known choruses; ask the members to suggest some they would like to sing.

Signify that the devotion is about to begin by reading John 21:1–10.

Then hand out the cooked fish and the bread or bread rolls. (If the fish is not cooked, sing another song or two.)

While the members are eating read John 21:11–14.

When the meal has been eaten the leader should get up and say to the members, 'Follow me'. Walk along the shore, making sure that the members stay together and can hear what is being said. Read John 21:15–19 while the group is walking along.

When the Bible reading is over, signif to the group that they are to sit down and quietly reflect on what Jesus mear when he says 'Follow me'.

Leader: The reading in John 21 talked about the meal those fishermen were sharing — the same meal we have shared today. Then the story continued about a man who came and invited those fishermen to follow him. And now Jesus invites us, too, to walk with him, to talk with him, to reflect on his place in our lives. He says 'Follow me'. What is your response? (Leave some time for reflection.)

Then pray: Lord, we are sometimes afraid to follow you, because we have to give so much of ourselves, and learn to be such different people. So help us in our struggles to walk in your footsteps. Help us to be your disciples. (Leave some time for silent prayer.) We ask all these things, knowing you are listening and understanding us. Amen.

Finish with this benediction: Jesus said to his disciples when he appeared to them after the resurrection, 'I have been given all authority in heaven and on earth. Go, then, to all peoples everywhere and make them my disciples: baptize them in the name of the Father, the Son, and the Holy Spirit, and teach them to obey everything I have commanded you. And I will be with you always, to the end of the age.' You go then and do the same. Amen.

Ian Crawford

EASTER IN RETROSPECT

(for use some time after Easter)

PREPARATION
You will need: a candle for every person in the group plus one extra, paper and pencils for every person.

DEVOTION

Have the members sitting in a circle, either on chairs or on the floor.

Explain in your own words Luke 24:13–24 as a way of setting the scene for the Bible reading. Then read Luke 24:25–35.

Leader: I'm going to invite you to think about Easter this year, what you did, how you celebrated it. I want you to think about the fact that Jesus died, went through agony, and was raised from the dead for us. (Leave time for reflection.)

Now I want you to think of the journey you have taken since Easter. Reflect on where you were at Easter, and where you have gone since then. If some resolutions were made this Easter, did you keep them? How? Why? If you didn't keep them, why didn't you?

Take time to think on it, and in so doing, take the time to think about the reason for Jesus' death on that cross and what that means for us today.

I invite you to represent your thoughts on paper, in pictures, words, poem, prose, whatever. It might represent your journey since Easter. *(Pass around the pencils and paper.)*

After sufficient time to complete this, invite the people to come back into the circle bringing the sheets with them. Put the sheets in the centre as an offering. Have a candle burning in the centre of the circle, representing Christ, and give each person a candle.

Leader: The offering you have just made is a symbol of our response to Jesus dying for us on the cross.

Now I want *(pick a person to start)* to light his/her candle from the Christ candle and in a few words recall what importance this Easter has played in his/her life. *(Allow a few moments for candle lighting and comments. Then ask that member to go and light the candle of someone else in the circle, who will respond with what importance this Easter has played in his/her life. Be aware that some may not want to respond; let them light their candles, then pass on to another person. When all candles are alight, have a time of silent reflection.)*

Sing a song about Jesus the light.

Conclude by reading John 17:1–5, 9–11.

Alison McRae

SUFFERING AT CHRISTMAS

PREPARATION

You will need: to cut out newspaper pictures of people dying, hungry, cold, troubled, etc. You will also need a member to read from the Bible.

DEVOTION

The leader begins in prayer: Lord, at Christmas time we look forward to the celebration, the good will, the gifts. Help us to remember most of all the gift you gave to us on that first Christmas, your Son Jesus. Amen.

The leader should recount to the group the story of the birth of Jesus, using either the gospel versions of the event, or your own words.

Have a member read Matthew 2:16–18.

Leader: With the birth of Jesus also came the death of all male children two years of age and under. Not much is said of the injustice of that act. God gave the world a Saviour and at the same time, one man — Herod — destroyed many lives.

When celebrating Christmas — Christ's coming —we must also mourn the death of so many innocent young children. Just as throughout the whole year we must remember the many innocent children, men and women who die in war or through starvation in the world.

Too often joyful events conveniently obscure the misery of death and suffering. Just as we celebrate the birth of Jesus and forget the slaughter of the innocents, we remember the victory of war and forget the homeless, orphaned, dead and injured children war creates.

This Christmas, let's remember the wonder of Christ, the love of God, but also remember the children of Bethlehem and their counterparts, the children of the 20th century. Perhaps we can find a way to support and help those who suffer all year round, we might decide to raise funds . . . (ask the members to suggest ways of aiding).

In this way only do we truly have the right to celebrate the coming of a man who stood for justice, kindness, love and peace, and who always stood by the side of the needy and the sick.

The leader should then hand out the newspaper cuttings to the members and have each person who gets a picture pray aloud for that situation.

Geraldine Anderson

PREPARE FOR THE MESSIAH

PREPARATION

You will need: a tape of 'Prepare ye the way of the Lord', and 'Day by day' from Godspell, a telephone (toy or real), taped sound of a telephone ringing, a member to act out a role play.

DEVOTION

Have the members sitting facing one focal point. Play the song 'Prepare ye the way of the Lord', up to but not including 'Day by day'.

Read Luke 2:1–7.

Play the taped telephone ringing, and have the member who is doing the role play go to answer the telephone.

Script

Hello *(pause)*
Who? *(pause)*
Oh! — God.
Well God, it certainly is nice of you to call — especially at Christmas time, what can I do for you? *(pause)*

What's that? *(pause)*

Well no, you can't come to **our** place. We've got all our relations coming over for lunch and dinner — mum couldn't cope with an extra. I'm sorry but there's just no room for you this Christmas. *(pause)*

Yes of course I remember the story, but we don't have a stable. *(pause)*

Look, be reasonable. It's my turn to play Santa for the little kids this year — I can't back out now. Anyway, what would Christmas be without Santa, I ask you? *(pause)*

Well, I guess you could try someone else. *(pause)* Well, Merry Christmas God — and ah, thanks again. *(pause)* You know, for the Messiah, peace on earth, good will and all that, we really appreciate it. *(hangs up)*

Play the song 'Day by day'.

Leader: As we come closer to Christmas, let's see if we can remember to keep God number one. Let's be ready for the anniversary of Jesus' birth, not the festivities of commercialised Christmas. Too often we celebrate Advent with the words 'Only ten more shopping days until Christmas', shouldn't we be saying, 'Only ten more days to prepare ourselves for the coming of our Lord?'

Let us pray: Lord, help us to be prepared when you call us. Help us to follow you day by day, from Christmas to Christmas and all the days in between. Amen.

Sing some Christmas carols.

Finish by reading John 3:16–17.

Geraldine Anderson

THE GIFT OF CHRISTMAS

PREPARATION
You will need: paper and coloured pencils or felt pens, enough for each person, some bright coloured Christmas paper, sticky tape, a box.

DEVOTION

Have the members either draw a picture or write a small poem or message wishing someone a merry Christmas. Explain to the members that they are to wrap up their drawings, poems or messages in the coloured Christmas paper and place them all in one box.

When this is done, get each member to take a 'present' from the box, making sure they don't get their own back. Ask them to open their 'presents', then find the person who made the 'present', thank him or her and sit down.

After settling the members read the following story:

About a month before Christmas each class in school drew names, to exchange gifts on the last day before the Christmas holiday. We seldom knew who our benefactor would be. I always hoped I would get a box of chocolate covered cherries — one of my very own. And the price was just right: forty nine cents, to meet our

fifty cent limit. But since the chocolate cherry box carried a telltale shape, I knew my wish had not been granted.

The box I got was long and flat. It was wrapped in plain white tissue paper with a slip of paper bearing my name. No ribbons or coloured paper, as on many gifts around me, but my present still intrigued me. What could be in such a large box yet weigh so little? A slight misgiving began to push into my mind. Why was the gift so plain? Why was it so light? Who had drawn my name? Not Anna — her presents were always wrapped beautifully. Not Alice — anybody could recognise her handwriting. Not Ronnie — he always gave chocolate covered cherries. Who then?

'To Grace from Mary.' My heart sank. It was the poorest child in the class. I lifted the lid of the box to find three items huddled together in a corner, dwarfed by the white emptiness around them. One was a gold pencil, without lead, and bearing a dent on one side. Another was a cardboard bookmark advertising a nearby funeral home and quoting a Bible verse of consolation. The third was a white handkerchief which had been carefully washed and ironed and folded in such a way as to hide a brownish stain that wouldn't quite come clean.

I felt shame, disappointment, hurt. I had nothing new and shiny to show. I thanked the giver, for I was polite, but in my heart I resented her for having drawn my name.

Looking back, I feel admiration for a mother who scraped together something for her child to give, a task that was multiplied by seven or eight other children. The little girl who carried the gift to school had to know her gift would pale beside the shiny gifts. Yet she offered it with dignity.

Ask the members to find the person who had made their gift and thank them again.

Have a member read Mark 12:41–44.

Finish by singing Christmas carols.

Geraldine Anderson

THE FLOOD

PREPARATION

You will need: pencil and paper for everyone, a member to read from the Bible.

DEVOTION

Distribute the pencils and paper. Then sing 'Noah and the flood' or another 'flood' song.

Signify that worship is to begin by having one or two minutes of silence.

Leader: The river around our homes is rising with flood waters. You are told it will be flooding three feet deep or more through your house within the hour. Write down in the order of importance from one to five what preparation you would make. Remember all the land around you is flat. (Leave about five minutes for the members to complete this.)

Ask the members to call out their lists (if time will allow).

Leader: Now that the flood is over and the water receded again, think about what is involved in the clean-up exercise. Discuss your future with two or three others around you. Place yourself totally in the situation and evaluate the smells, feelings, sights and sounds (Give about three minutes for this exercise.)

Have a member read Matthew 24:36–44.

Leader: You have heard Christ is coming again soon. What preparations will you make? (Give about two minutes contemplative silence.)

Close in prayer: Lord, we come before you in prayer, asking for your help in all we do. Help us in our lives always to be prepared for you, always seeing you in other people who are in need, unhappy, hungry, cold. We will try to be ready for you when you come. Help us, Lord, to be your children. Amen.

Anne Harley

UNITY

PREPARATION

You will need: a pencil and some paper for each person in the group, a member to read from the Bible.

DEVOTION

Have the group sit in a circle. Give each person a pencil and some paper.

Allow some time for silence, then signify that the devotion is to begin by saying a brief prayer: Lord, we come before you, knowing that you love us; help us to be open to your spirit. Amen.

Ask each person to draw on the piece of paper a symbol of how they feel at this moment — a symbol, word or drawing which represents them at this time. Tell the members that they will not have to explain what they draw to anybody else. When they finish, ask them to place their pieces of paper in the middle of the circle.

Walk into the centre of the circle while a member reads Ephesians 2:1–5. Slowly move the pieces of paper around so as to roughly form the shape of a cross. The person reading the Bible passage will probably need to read it through again to allow you sufficient time to form the cross shape.

Leader: This group is made up of different people, with different needs and personalities, as shown by the different symbols drawn on the pieces of paper in the middle of the circle.

Although we are all different, to God all the people in this group are equally important.

The cross in the middle of the circle represents Jesus Christ, who binds all of the members of our group together.

Because we are all bound together by the cross, we have a responsibility to care for each other. Some people here may be happy, some probably sad, some possibly hurting about all sorts of things. As God cares for us, so we need to care for each other as responsible Christian group members.

Have all the members hold hands while still sitting in the circle and sing a song about unity and being one in the Spirit.

Grant Nichol

WORSHIPPING WITH THE FIRST CHRISTIANS

PREPARATION
You will need: a candle.

This devotion relies on the members of your group. You will have to ask them to tell stories, suggest songs to sing. Perhaps you might like to inform two or three people about what you are going to do, so they will be able to help you keep the devotion flowing.

DEVOTION

Have the members sit on the floor in a circle. Set the candle in the centre of the circle. Turn the lights off, and leave a little time for reflective silence.

Leader: When the first Christians met, they had to meet in secret, because they were not welcome in the synagogues and it was against the law for them to meet and worship. They probably met in dark, secluded caves, early in the morning or late at night. Their worship was much the same as the worship we have now, except they didn't have hymn books, or music, nothing written down about the life of Jesus. They had to rely on either eyewitness accounts or stories passed on from people about what Jesus did and said. They relied on their memories of Jesus and worshipped simply and with hardly any aids. They would spontaneously pray about their concerns and needs, share stories, sit in silence, join in singing, teach, ask questions etc.

In this devotion we are going to do the same sort of things they did. We won't use hymn books or Bibles, song sheets or music. It is possible to worship in this way because basically, our worship will have the same elements in it as any other act of worship, we will just be relying on our memories in all that we do.

Could someone suggest a song everyone would know well? (This is where your primed people come in, to help if no-one is willing to suggest a song.)

Could someone tell us something they remember of what Jesus has said, or done? Perhaps you know of a story that has affected you and you would like to share it? (Leave time for a few stories.)

Does anyone want to ask any questions about these stories? Is anything unclear to anyone? (Leave time for questions.)

Could someone suggest another song? Something everyone will know well.

Now let's thank God for this time together. We'll have an open prayer of thanksgiving. An open prayer is when we leave the prayer open for those who would like to pray out loud. Let us pray. (Leave sufficient time for the prayer. Don't worry about long silences — the members may want to pray silently. However, here again the people you have primed may be able to help out.)

Could someone suggest another song?

We will finish this time of worship with a prayer. Could everyone hold the hand of the person next to them. Let us pray: Father, we thank you for

enabling us to spend this time together, without fear of being persecuted. We thank you for those brave first Christians who paved the way for us. We thank you for the stories, the songs, the silence we have shared with you in this time. Be with us as we resume our 20th century lives, guide us and support us. Amen.

Geraldine Anderson

YOU'VE GOT A FRIEND

PREPARATION
Arrange for some slides to be taken of the youth group sharing in fun or fellowship, or use slides group members may have taken.

Find a recording of Carole King's song 'You've got a friend'. It is on her album Tapestry *and on the album* The Best of James Taylor *by James Taylor.*

You will need: slides, projector, screen, tape or record, tape recorder or stereo, newsprint and pens or chalkboard and chalk.

DEVOTION

Show the slides while playing the song 'You've got a friend . Let the group see

each slide for at least five to ten seconds.

Divide the group into smaller groups of five to six. Have these questions written on newsprint and then ask the group to discuss them.
> What does the word 'friendship' mean to you?
> Who do you turn to when you are 'down and troubled'?
> Do you turn to God for help when you are 'down and troubled'? Why? Why not?

Call the group back together again. Choose one of the best slides to show on the screen. Leave it on, and read Psalm 23:1–4.

Close with silent prayer for each member of the group. Either say the name of each person aloud, or show the slides again.

Geraldine Anderson